This book belongs to

....

This is the story of a man named Noah.

Read it yourself – go on, have a go-ah!

There's something else. Can you guess what?

On every page there's a hammer to spot.

This edition first published in the UK in 2006 by Authentic Media

Copyright © 2006 make believe ideas ltd.

27 Castle Street, Berkhamsted, Herts, HP4 2DW

Text copyright © 2006 Nick and Claire Page

Manufactured in China.

Noah
and the
Ark

Nick and Claire Page

Illustrations by Helen Parrott

A
Authentic

God said to Noah: "Build me a boat;
Build me a box and make it float.
Throughout the earth there is evil and pain;
I'm going to wash everywhere clean again."

Noah said to God: "Well, what about me?
I have a lovely wife and family.
I've never ever stepped in a boat before;
I can't use a sail and I can't row an oar."

God said to Noah:

"You're a very good man.
You and your family are part of my plan.
Take them on board and don't get stressed.
Just stick to floating. I'll do the rest."

So Noah started hammering,
Noah started nailing,
Before it started showering,
Before it started hailing.

He kept looking up, expecting to get wet,
But the rain didn't come. At least, not yet...

God said to Noah: "Build me a zoo.
Fill it with animals, two by two.
I'll send you every animal under the sun
Just keep them dry, until I'm done."

Noah said to God: "You're having a laugh!
I've never had a puppy, let alone a giraffe.
How will I feed them? My mind's in a blur!
I've never run a zoo: I'm allergic to fur!"

God said to Noah: "Don't you fret,
There's room enough for everyone –
you won't get wet.
Pretty soon now, the rain will fall,
And then it will be curtains for one and all."

So Noah started painting,
Noah started sawing,
Before it started showering,
Before it started pouring.

He was just finishing work on his floating zoo,
When the animals arrived, two by two...

And there were...
Ants and bees and cats and dogs,
Elephants, foxes, goats and hogs,
Iguanas, jackals, koalas, lice,
Every single animal came on twice!

There were...

Monkeys, newts, okapis, pandas,

Quaggas, roosters, salamanders,

Toads, umbrella birds, voles, wallaroo,

Xemes and yaks and two zebu!

DO NOT DISTURB

LEVEL
1   2   3

Every animal you ever knew –
All in Noah's floating zoo!

God said to Noah: "Get on board,
The world's going to feel
the power of the Lord!
Close all the hatches, shut the door.
Hold on tight, it's about to pour!"

The boat started sailing,
Animals were roaring,
Water started rising,
Rain it came a-pouring.

It rained for forty days without a break,
The world turned into a great big lake.

Noah said to God: "We're in good shape.
But I'm worried that the woodworms
are trying to escape.
The hippo's got a toothache,
the lion's lost his roar..."
God said: "Send the raven
to see if there's a shore."

18

So Noah sent the raven,
but no luck there –
Too much water everywhere;
Then he sent a dove,
but that came back too,
There was nowhere to land,
except the floating zoo.

Noah waited a while, then sent the dove south,
It came back later with a leaf in its mouth.
"Aha!" said Noah. "The water's gone down.
It's OK, folks, we're not going to drown!"

LEAF
RECOGNITION
MADE
EASY

So he waited some more,
then set the dove free,
This time the bird
found a home in a tree.
It never came back to old Noah's hand,
For it had found a better place to land.

The ark ran aground on a mountain top,
And there the adventure came to a stop.
Noah looked out: the land was dry below,
So he opened the door and let the creatures go.

God said to Noah: "No, never again,
Will I wash this world with flood and rain.
I promise you, Noah, and my promise is true,
From this day on, I'll always be with you."

Skies started brightening,
Flowers started budding,
God made a promise:
No more flooding.

He painted his promise across the sky
A beautiful rainbow, way up high.
Lots of love,
God.

Ready to tell

Oh no! Some of the pictures from this story have been mixed up! Can you retell the story and point to each picture in the correct order?

Picture dictionary

Encourage your child to read these harder words from the story and gradually develop their basic vocabulary.

animals

ark

dove

Noah

rain

raven

sky

tree

water

I • up • look • we • like • and • on • at • for

Key words

Here are some key words used in context. Help your child to use other words from the border in simple sentences.

Noah built **a** boat.

The animals went on the ark.

It began to rain.

He can **see** dry land.

All the animals were safe.

a • he • is • said • go • you • are • this • going • they • away • play • cat • to

am • can • yes • it • see • she • me • of • was • went • in • come • get • day

the • dog • big • my • mum • no • dad • all

Make a rainbow cake!

Hold a rainbow party to celebrate the happy ending to Noah's story – and serve this scrummy rainbow cake!

You will need

a large round cake (homemade or bought) • ½ cup soft margarine • 1½ cups sieved icing sugar • 4 tbsp milk • 2 tsp vanilla • blue and green food colouring • mixing bowl • large spoon or spatula • two packets of chocolate beans

What to do

1 Put the cake on a large plate or board.

2 Mix all the ingredients except the colouring together until smooth. Divide this icing into two batches.

3 Mix one batch with a drop or two of blue colouring to make sky-coloured icing. Spread this over half the cake with the back of the spoon or spatula.

4 Mix the rest of the icing with a drop of green colouring to make grass-coloured icing. Spread this over the other half of the cake. Put the cake to one side.

5 Do you know the colours of the rainbow? (See page 31.) Sort the chocolate beans into groups of these colours.

6 Not long before eating, arrange the chocolate beans on the blue icing to make a rainbow. (You'll have to miss out indigo.) Serve and enjoy!